Keep Your Pantheon

(and School)

TWO UNRELATED PLAYS

OTHER BOOKS BY DAVID MAMET
PUBLISHED BY TCG

Race

Keep Your Pantheon

(and School)

TWO UNRELATED PLAYS

David Mamet

THEATRE COMMUNICATIONS GROUP
NEW YORK
2012

Keep Your Pantheon (and School): Two Unrelated Plays is published by Theatre Communications Group, Inc., 520 Eighth Avenue, 24th Floor, New York, NY 10018-4156

The publication of *Keep Your Pantheon (and School): Two Unrelated Plays* by David Mamet, through TCG's Book Program, is made possible in part by the New York State Council on the Arts with the support of Governor Andrew Cuomo and the New York State Legislature.

TCG books are exclusively distributed to the book trade by Consortium Book Sales and Distribution.

LIBRARY OF CONGRESS CATALOGING-IN-PUBLICATION DATA
Mamet, David.
Keep your pantheon (and School) : two unrelated plays / David Mamet.
—1st ed.
p. cm.
ISBN 978-1-55936-391-4
I. Mamet, David. School. II. Title. III. Title: School.
PS3563.A4345K444   2011
812'.54—dc23   2011040062

Book design and composition by Lisa Govan
Cover illustration by David Mamet
Cover design by Lisa Govan

First Edition, April 2012

Contents

Keep Your Pantheon

This play is dedicated to Jack Wallace

Keep Your Pantheon premiered in May 2008 at the Center Theatre Group (Michael Ritchie, Artistic Director; Charles Dillingham, Managing Director) in Los Angeles. It was performed as a double bill with *The Duck Variations*. It was directed by Neil Pepe. Set design was by Takeshi Kata, costume design was by Ilona Somogyi, lighting design was by Christopher Akerlind and sound design was by Cricket S. Myers. The production stage manager was David S. Franklin and the stage manager was Elizabeth Atkinson. The cast was as follows:

HERALD	Vincent Guastaferro
STRABO	Ed O'Neill
PELARGON	David Paymer
PHILIUS	Michael Cassidy
RAMUS	Jack Wallace
QUINTUS MAGNUS	Steven Goldstein
TITUS	J. J. Johnston
LUPUS ALBUS	Dominic Hoffman
MESSENGER	Rod McLachlan
ENSEMBLE	Jeffrey Addiss, Rod McLachlan, Jonathan Rossetti

Keep Your Pantheon was produced in September 2009 at Atlantic Theater Company (Neil Pepe, Artistic Director; Jeffory Lawson, Managing Director) in New York City. It was performed as a double bill with *School*. It was directed by Neil Pepe. Set design was by

Takeshi Kata, costume design was by Ilona Somogyi and lighting design was by Christopher Akerlind. The production stage manager was Gregory T. Livoti. The cast was as follows:

HERALD	Steven Hawley
STRABO	Brian Murray
PELARGON	John Pankow
PHILIUS	Michael Cassidy
RAMUS	Jack Wallace
QUINTUS MAGNUS	Todd Weeks
TITUS	J. J. Johnston
LUPUS ALBUS	Jordan Lage
MESSENGER	Rod McLachlan
ENSEMBLE	Jeffrey Addiss, Rod McLachlan, Jonathan Rossetti

CHARACTERS

HERALD

STRABO: An actor

PELARGON: An actor

PHILIUS: Strabo's young apprentice

RAMUS: An old drunk

QUINTUS MAGNUS: The landlord

MESSENGER

MAN

AUDIENCE

TITUS: A jailor

LUPUS ALBUS: The White Wolf of Phrygia, a general

CENTURIONS

ARMORERS

GUARDS

PRIEST

SETTING

Ancient Rome.

The impatient crowd rushed at the dawn of day to secure their places, and there were many who passed a sleepless and anxious night in the adjacent porticos. From the morning to the evening, careless of the sun, or of the rain, the spectators, who sometimes amounted to the number of four hundred thousand, remained in eager attention.

—Edward Gibbon,
The History of the Decline and Fall of the Roman Empire

Scene One

An actors' studio in ancient Rome. Two actors, Strabo and Pelargon, in ratty clothes, are batting their arms, trying to keep warm. Walking up and down.
Outside, in the rain, a Herald walks by the open windows.

HERALD:
>O for the tongues of all the gods
>To decry that fate, which 'gainst all odds
>Has brought the Tenth African Legion low
>Oh, Rome, rend your garments and ashes throw . . .

STRABO: Has anybody seen my codpiece? . . .

HERALD:
>Has brought the Tenth African
>Legion low . . .

PELARGON *(To the Herald)*: Hey, what happened to the Tenth African Legion?

HERALD:
> The Tenth African Legion has suffered its first defeat . . .

STRABO: Mee, me, mo mo moo moo . . . Has anybody seen my codpiece? . . .

HERALD:
> They have suffered their first defeat
> Loss is more bitter than victory's sweet.

STRABO: Mmee mee hah mah . . . Would you, *would* you, give a work-
ing man a break.

HERALD: Buy Sosostris Sandals—the Egyptians wore them. They
just don't wear out!

STRABO: Has anybody—

PELARGON: You don't need your codpiece to do your voice exercises.

STRABO: I don't work without my codpiece.

PELARGON: The kid is not going to be impressed by your codpiece.

STRABO: Where is he?

PELARGON: He went out to get the mail.

STRABO: IN THE RAIN? YOU LET HIM GO OUT IN THE
RAIN?

(The kid, Philius, enters sopping wet and sneezes.)

PHILIUS: Achoo.

STRABO: Young Philius, may I assist you out of those wet clothes? . . .

PELARGON *(To self)*: . . . Oh, please.

(Philius sneezes.)

STRABO: And are you unwell?

PHILIUS *(Quoting)*: "What is the health of this mineral body, com-
pared to the health of Rome?"

STRABO: That's *very* good.

PELARGON: It's "mortal body," not "mineral body."

STRABO: He *said* "mortal body."

PELARGON: I can't understand a thing he's saying.

STRABO: He's getting a *cold*, all right? And P.S. any *dolt* can *say the
words. He's* got the *feeling.*

(Philius sneezes.)

Give him a cup of wine.

PELARGON: It's our last wine.

STRABO: And are we not to share it with our *student?* With that youth who has so esteemed us, as to leave his home, and apply to us for instruction? . . . Who has thrown his lot in with us. In pursuit of that Most Noble of Achievements: Service of *Thalia*, the Muse of Comedy. God *bless* you, youngster. How it delights these old bones to feel the *warmth* of your enthusiasms. May our years together . . .

(Philius shows a letter.)

PHILIUS: Strabo, I have a letter for you.

STRABO: Who is the letter from?

PHILIUS: My father.

STRABO: Ah. And did he send money?

PHILIUS: No. He says I have to come home.

(Pause.)

STRABO: Why?

PHILIUS: Because, you said you'd put me on the stage—and since I've arrived, you haven't had a job.

(Pause.)

And you said you'd put me onstage.

STRABO: And I *shall* put you onstage. WHERE YOU BELONG. *But.* One must have patience.

PHILIUS: And we don't have enough to eat.

STRABO: It's the Spartan Method. We've explained the Spartan Method.

PHILIUS *(As water falls on his head)*: And the roof is leaking.

STRABO: Philius, the service of our Muse is hard. But Fortune favors fortitude. How we will laugh, in times to come at what will, in that happy hour, be seen as less than inconveniences.

PHILIUS: Oh, and I have another letter.

STRABO *(As Philius hands him the letter)*: What is it?

PELARGON (*Reads*): It's an inquiry of our availability.

STRABO: An inquiry of our availability. You see! You see! We *are* available. The day is *saved*. Fortune has smiled on our steadfastness. *Write* your father. Tell him we are employed.

PHILIUS: I'm happy, Strabo.

STRABO: I know that you are. See how the merest brief emotions pursue each other o'er the bright plasticity of his manly face.

(It rains on them.)

PHILIUS: Should I go up and fix the leak?

PELARGON: How would you fix it?

PHILIUS: I could find out where it's coming from.

PELARGON: I believe it's coming from the roof.

PHILIUS: I believe so, too. "And I praise Mighty Zeus, for that bright happy wind which . . ."

PELARGON: ". . . steered me . . ."

STRABO: *He* knows it . . . *he* knows it . . .

PHILIUS: ". . . steered me to this refuge. O Athena, send your seed of wisdom to search through the rock of my innards."

PELARGON: Amen, with all my heart.

(Philius exits.)

STRABO: The lad *has* something—don't you think?

PELARGON: He'll never go to bed with you.

STRABO: His reluctance, to date, I lay at the feet of poverty. *(Taking the letter)* With the belly full "love will bloom like the wild gorse on Mount Ida." The Sicilian Cork Festival!!!

PELARGON *(Taking back the letter)*: The *Lesser* Sicilian Cork Festival.

STRABO: Are not the Lesser Sicilians entitled to amusement? . . . When does our engagement begin?

PELARGON: It's not an engagement. It's an *audition*.

STRABO: An audition . . . ?

PELARGON: Yes.

STRABO: They want me to come to Sicily to *audition*?

PELARGON *(Reads; showing the letter)*: "The proctors of the Lesser Sicilian Cork Festival are pleased to announce that you have been selected as one of the *thirty* troops invited to audition . . ."

STRABO: I? *Strabo?*

PELARGON: *Yes.*

STRABO: *Strabo?* Who played before Caesar . . . ?

PELARGON: . . . as a child . . .

STRABO: Who reduced the Neapolitan Senate to tears . . .

PELARGON *(Simultaneously):* . . . reduced the Neapolitan Senate to tears . . .

STRABO: To whom, this gifted lad, this *comet*, has applied for instruction? He *could* have gone to the Company of Paulus, may his name be accursed. No. But he did not *go* to the Company of Paulus. No—he came *here* . . . to work beneath me . . .

PELARGON: Dream on.

STRABO: And, these *swine* ask me: to "audition," to "plead," to be allowed to play the . . . *what* is it?

PELARGON: . . . the Lesser Sicilian.

STRABO: The Lesser Sicilian *Cork* Festival? While Paulus, *that hack*, in my rightful place, performs before Caesar.

PELARGON: Well, not now he doesn't, 'cause he's in Sardinia.

STRABO: May he remain there. Entertaining savages.

(The door opens. Ramus, an old drunk, enters.)

RAMUS: By the gods.

PELARGON: By the gods.

STRABO: Not today.

RAMUS: I seek no charity . . . I come with . . .

STRABO: Yes, I know. Charms and portents, potions and news. Not tod—

RAMUS: A love charm . . .

STRABO: I don't require a love charm.

RAMUS: I saw the kid on the roof.

STRABO: I don't require a love charm to succeed with the kid.

RAMUS: How long's he been with you?

STRABO: He's *shy*, all right, the lad's shy . . .

(Ramus displays the various tchotchkes hung on his belt.)

RAMUS: A fetish, a *token*, which I will *trade*, for one cup of wine.

STRABO: Absolutely not.

RAMUS: I have a *token* to dispel bad luck.

STRABO: No.

RAMUS: One cup of wine . . .

STRABO: Go away.

RAMUS: *This charm* was given to me, by the Great Lupus Albus, White Wolf of Sardinia, when we served in the Tenth African Legion.

STRABO: You served in the Tenth African Legion?

RAMUS: I served beside him. In the snows.

PELARGON: What was the Tenth African Legion doing in the snows?

RAMUS: We were lost. *(Pause)* And I need a drink.

STRABO: That's quite a shock.

RAMUS: Because I'm having a particularly hard day.

PELARGON: Why is that?

RAMUS: *Because* I have just heard they have suffered defeat.

STRABO: Who has suffered defeat?

RAMUS: The Tenth African Legion. My comrades . . . have suffered their first defeat . . .

STRABO: You were never in the Tenth African Legion.

PHILIUS *(Reentering; drenched)*: Strabo . . .

STRABO *(To Philius)*: You look lovely when you're wet.

PHILIUS: Thank you, Strabo.

STRABO: What did you want to tell me?

PHILIUS: The landlord's coming.

PELARGON: Oh, no.

PHILIUS *(Exiting)*: I'm going to change my clothes.

STRABO *(To Philius)*: Put on something revealing.

(The landlord, Quintus Magnus, enters.)

QUINTUS: By the gods.

PELARGON: By the gods.

STRABO *(To Ramus)*: We are honored, sir. We are honored. That you chose us.

QUINTUS: Strabo.

STRABO: Quintus. You shouldn't be out in this weather. One moment— *(To Ramus)* Chose *us*, sir, over . . . *(To Quintus)* He could have hired the Troop of Paulus.

QUINTUS: Strabo . . .

STRABO: He could have hired the Troop of Paulus, beloved of Caesar . . .

QUINTUS: Strabo.

STRABO: But this man of taste chose *us.*

QUINTUS: Your rent is four months overdue . . .

STRABO: We would have brought it to you, but for this accursed rain . . .

QUINTUS: *I* came out in the rain . . .

STRABO: You're a bold man, and I applaud you for it.

PHILIUS *(Returning; a towel over his head)*: Achoo.

QUINTUS: The child looks *dreadful* . . .

STRABO: I would have come, even *given* the rain—but for my understandable anxiety. My new lead, here, young Philius, has caught a cold. Which, Zeus forfend, might *might* prohibit him from performing in the upcoming festival for which we've been engaged.

QUINTUS: You've got a job?

STRABO: This, this man of discernment has come to engage us to open the Sicilian Cork Festival.

(Pause.)

QUINTUS: The Sicilian Cork Festival . . .

STRABO: The honorarium for which will, thank you for waiting, discharge our debts, and restore my troupe, in the eyes of the world, to that position it deserves.

QUINTUS: You're going to sail to Sicily?

STRABO: In his private trireme.

QUINTUS: This fellow looks like a beggar.

STRABO: Which disguise, sir, has kept him safe, rich as he is, rich as Marcus Rufus *Cronax*, through travels, through his vast possessions, throughout the Known World. *Thank* you for waiting, Quintus.

PHILIUS: We're going to Sicily, Strabo . . . ?

QUINTUS: Before you go, would you pay the rent?

STRABO: Upon the instant. Let me but collect an advance upon the swingeing fee this fine man has offered.

(They turn to Ramus, who is now asleep. Pause.)

Hush, thinking again. Do not wake him. For he has come, battered by the storm, from far-off Sicily. And the journey has fatigued him. Let our benefactor sleep. Sleep on, oh Patron of the Arts.

QUINTUS: Fifty sesterces. Tomorrow morning.

STRABO: When I shall come, sir, with this good man's "stipend," in my pocket placing it, *gently*, no, but not without a sense of triumph, in your sweating hands.

QUINTUS: Or, I'm going to sic the bailiffs on you.

STRABO: How we'll laugh, tomorrow morning. Recalling those intemperate words . . .

QUINTUS: By the gods.

PELARGON: By the gods.

(Quintus exits into the storm.)

PHILIUS: We're going to Sicily, Strabo? . . .

STRABO *(To Pelargon)*: Wake him up.

PHILIUS: Because, if we are, I'm going to need some new clothes.

PELARGON: What is our plan? . . .

STRABO: It's not a "plan," Pelargon. It is known as a "plot." Which, as we are taught, is based upon human *motivation*.

PELARGON: And what is the motivation?

STRABO: *Greed.* Tomorrow *morning* . . .

PELARGON: Tomorrow morning, the landlord doesn't get the rent, we go to debtor's prison.

STRABO: I shall give him something rather *better* than the rent.

PELARGON: What?

STRABO: "An unexpected *windfall*." What man does not *prize* "an unexpected windfall"?

PELARGON: What is the windfall?

STRABO: We offer to *buy his building*. Ramus, this insanely wealthy gentleman from Sicily, offers to buy this pest-trap for some fabulous sum . . . *(To Ramus)* Wake up.

PELARGON: And how do we pay for it?

STRABO: For what?

PELARGON: The building.

STRABO: Negotiations for the building, listen and learn, "drag on for months," this is called "buying time," during which time . . . *(To Ramus)* Wake up.

RAMUS *(Waking)*: Trinkets, potions and news. I do not seek charity . . .

STRABO: Ramus, we have a job for you.

RAMUS: Make a small purchase. From an old soldier . . .

STRABO: Raa . . .

PELARGON: Buy something . . .

PHILIUS: Buy a charm, buy a charm, Strabo.

STRABO: Yes, yes, yes, *Ramus*. Oh, please. This charm, sell me this charm. *(He points to a charm hanging on Ramus's belt)*

RAMUS: A fine choice, sir, for *that* charm was a gift from Lupus Albus, the White Wolf of Sardinia, when we served in . . .

STRABO AND RAMUS *(Simultaneously)*: . . . the Tenth African Legion.

RAMUS: Which charm is warranted to immediately reverse ill fortune.

STRABO: Accept this small coin with my thanks. Ramus: tomorrow morning, we're going to put on a little "play" . . . *You* will impersonate a Sicilian lord . . .

PELARGON: How're we going to pass him off as a Sicilian lord?

STRABO *(Stating the obvious)*: We're going to show up with him drunk. As drunk as one after a night touring "Rome's curious byways . . ." So drunk will he be that, in his drunkenness, he wants to buy this *pest-hole* for five times its worth.

PELARGON: Why?

(Pause.)

STRABO: It reminds him of his aunt's house in Sardinia.

PHILIUS: You're very smart, Strabo.

STRABO: Study the Classics. —Now, Ramus . . .

(A knocking is heard at the door. All turn. Philius goes to the door.)

VOICE *(Offstage)*: Open up!

STRABO: Oh, no.

PHILIUS: Who could be coming out in such a storm?

PELARGON: The bailiffs.

STRABO: The swine actually *sent* the bailiffs.
VOICE *(Offstage)*: Open up!
STRABO: All right. Tell them . . . *tell* them, we've gone.
PHILIUS: Where have we gone?
STRABO: To the Sicilian Cork Festival.
PELARGON: "Just when everything was going so well . . ."

(Philius opens the door. A Messenger stands in the doorway.)

MESSENGER: By the gods.
PELARGON: Oh, all right.
PHILIUS: Be welcome. To the Studio of Strabo. Sicily called them and they have responded, and, thus, are not here. *(Pause)* Belike they are elsewhere.

(Pause.)

MESSENGER: *What* did you say?
STRABO: He said "the Studio of Strabo."
MESSENGER: Why does he talk like that?
STRABO: He has a cold.
MESSENGER: He said "the Studio of Strabo"?
STRABO: Yes.
MESSENGER: I *seek* the Studio of Strabo.
STRABO: You found it, but they aren't here.
MESSENGER: I had difficulty locating your house in the storm.
STRABO: A bailiff may not evict lawful tenants from their home between dusk and dawn.
MESSENGER: I'm . . .
STRABO: Tell him.
PELARGON: Section Three of the Pandects of Justinian.

(Pelargon shrugs: "I'm making it up, but who's gonna check?")

MESSENGER: I've studied the Pandects of Justinian.
STRABO: As who has not.
MESSENGER: And I don't seem to . . .
STRABO: Get on with it.
MESSENGER: I represent Marcus Rufus Cronax. Richest man in Rome.

(Pause.)

STRABO: Marcus Cronax. Richest man in Rome?
MESSENGER: As I have said. Who had engaged an acting troupe. To perform this evening at his wife's festivities. They are unable to perform, and he sends to ask you to appear in their stead.

(Pause.)

The fee is meager, but six hundred sesterces, however . . .
STRABO: You wish us to perform *tonight* . . .
MESSENGER: We had engaged the Company of Gaius Paulus . . .
STRABO: You had engaged the Company of Gaius Paulus . . .
MESSENGER: But they have been lost at sea.

(Pause.)

STRABO: Oh gods, oh gods of fate, how we, from one dark moment to the next, stumble, grope and curse that which, with trust in *you* is revealed as a clear, shining path.
PELARGON: We'll be there.
MESSENGER: The loss of brother actors must come as a cruel shock . . .
STRABO: Paulus? Drowned? Where may we seek for consolation? . . .
MESSENGER: Paulus. Yes. And all his company . . .
PELARGON: *Incredible* loss to the theatrical world.
MESSENGER: . . . the favorite actors of Caesar . . .
STRABO: After the engagement we will rend our flesh.
MESSENGER: Here are a list of the topics, they were to have dealt with at tonight's festivities . . . We have but the one question . . .
STRABO: State it.
MESSENGER: . . . Do you have *time* enough, to fashion a play, between now and sunset? . . .
STRABO: Sir, I am Strabo, who once improvised a two-hour ode . . .
MESSENGER: Oh. Where?

(Pause.)

PELARGON: At the Sicilian Cork Festival.

STRABO *(To Pelargon)*: Thank you.

MESSENGER: Here is the list of suggested topics. Do you know the house?

STRABO: Do I know the *house?*

MESSENGER: It is right next to the *armory.*

STRABO: Who does not know the house of Marcus Rufus Cronax!

MESSENGER: We expect you at sunset.

STRABO: Can the sand stop the tide? . . .

MESSENGER: By the gods.

STRABO: Let us praise them with all our being.

(The Messenger exits.)

(Does a "stop the music") Oh, ye gods, full of compassion who mete out to man not by his deserts, but by your immutable weights of Justice. Oh, ye gods, who *do* exist . . .

PHILIUS: But . . .

STRABO: . . . grant that the Troupe of Gaius Paulus, now taken to you, expired in prolonged agony.

PHILIUS: . . . but.

STRABO: . . . in the raging sea. —What?

PHILIUS: But are we going to Sicily, Strabo?

STRABO: No, sweetheart, we're going to stay here and get rich.

Scene Two

A street. Night. Rain. The Herald walks by.

HERALD:
>The Tenth African Legion in ignominy shamed.
>Then the Troupe of Paulus drowned at sea.
>The gods bid Rome within its doors to keep.
>Whilst the skies visage clouds,
>And een the heavens weep, oh woe, oh woe.

(The Herald passes by as the three actors take shelter beneath an overhang. Strabo is doing his vocal exercises.)

STRABO *(To the Herald)*: Oh, take it elsewhere.

HERALD: Peloponnesian Syrup of Myrtle—Rectifies the humors. *Patricians* use it, *you* can use it, too! Peloponnesian Syrup of Myrtle—Ask for it by name.

STRABO: Mee mee mma maaa, mo mo mooo moo . . .

PELARGON *(Reading from a list)*: Topics to be covered at tonight's festivities.

STRABO: *Test* me, I am prepared . . .

PELARGON: Cronax: his opposition, in the Senate, to the African Campaign.

STRABO: The Tenth African Legion, we see, has just suffered its first defeat, as predicted, *predicted*, mind you, *in* the Senate, by our host, Marcus Rufus Cronax, arch *foe* of the Tenth African Legion . . .

PELARGON: . . . which brings us . . .

STRABO: I've got it. *I've* got it . . .

PHILIUS: What do I get to say, Strabo . . .

STRABO: I've got it, which, naturally, takes me to . . . *which* is the house, now? . . .

(All look around.)

PELARGON: It's around here somewhere . . .

STRABO: Which brings us to . . . his "tastes" . . . our host, and his "curious tastes."

PELARGON: You're cutting pretty close to the bone.

STRABO: Cronax is *famed*, all right? For enjoying a bawdy joke at his own expense. He's got a heart as big as the Coliseum, which is now under construction. *(Pause)* All right? Our host, who, as we know, has developed a "certain proclivity" . . . I'm not going to say that he "likes *women*," but, it's been noted that he goes to bed with people who are "lacking in exterior equipment . . ." Uh . . . "Tenth African *Legion*" . . . favorite of Caesar . . . likes "women" . . .

PELARGON: I'm not sure you can say that and get away with it.

STRABO: "Grasp fortune by the forelock, Pelargon, for she has no hair behind."

(A door opens before them and a Man peers out.)

Ah. Here we are . . .

(The actors enter a darkened room lit by torchlight.)

By the gods.

MAN: By the gods!

STRABO: We have arrived.

MAN: We feared the storm would hinder you.

STRABO: I hope my troupe, sir, knows its duty.

MAN: Bless you.

STRABO: We live to serve.

MAN: Shall I present you? . . .

STRABO: No, no, why win them over *twice*? You leave the evening in my hands.

(The Man leads them to a small dais, before which sits ten men. Strabo takes the stage.)

PHILIUS: Strabo . . .

STRABO: Not now. —*Gentlemen*. Sorry if we're late. I'm not going to tell you that it's *wet*, but I got a *squid* down my shirt.

(Pause.)

And I'd complain, except he was giving me a *hickey* . . .

(Pause.)

He was giving me a *hickey*. I, uh . . . I know, I've got to be careful, touching on *personal* matters. I know our *host*, for example, has, and god knows he's entitled to them, "curious tastes" . . . I'm not saying he likes "women," but . . . But we know some of the people he goes to bed with are noticeably lacking in exterior equipment. Or, as the soldiers say, "Perhaps they forgot to pack their tent pole."

(Deathly silence.)

". . . pack their tent pole . . ." We're told he made the switch to *women* and on his *wedding* night uttered that timeless phrase: "I know it's around here *somewhere* . . ." He's had three wives—but that may be because he thought the clitoris was a building in *Greece*.

(Pause.)

PELARGON *(Prompting)*: Tenth African Legion . . .

PHILIUS: Strabo . . .

STRABO: Speaking of which, I see where, "too bad," the Tenth African Legion has suffered its first defeat. You know who *they* are. *They're* the boys their spears come in three sizes: small, medium and "thank you for a lovely evening."

PHILIUS: Strabo.

(Pause.)

STRABO: I see they got their asses whomped and they've been brought home in *shame.* Well, what general planned that campaign? He must be one arch shy of an aqueduct . . .

(Pause.)

. . . one arch shy of an aqueduct . . .

(The audience grumbles.)

Well, *they'll* have less heads, but *we'll* have more helmets . . .

PHILIUS: Strabo, we're in the wrong house.

(The audience grumbles.)

Cronax lives across the street.

AUDIENCE MEMBER: Kill them all!

PHILIUS: This is the Armory of the Tenth African Legion . . .

AUDIENCE: *Kill* them, *kill* them, *kill* them! . . .

(Blackout. The Herald enters.
The dungeon room of the Tenth African Legion. Night. Philius,
Pelargon and Strabo are chained to a bench.)

HERALD:

    O Wicked wicked world
    How you have wronged me
    For my love lies 'crost the
    Straits of Messina
    O, Fortunate, you pelicans and other wingèd birds

Original verses—no two alike—
Or will write-to-suit—
You only pay for what you use—
Original verses—
We come to you—

STRABO: Well, there's some *mistake*.

(Titus walks by.)

Fellow.

TITUS: What?
STRABO: Fellow, there's some mistake.
TITUS: Well, no. I know that.
STRABO: And I'd like to *ask* you, to bring down, someone in *charge*.
So that we may correct this unfortunate misunderstanding.
Who's in charge here?
TITUS: Lupus Albus.
STRABO: Lupus Albus? The White Wolf of Sardinia? . . .
TITUS: No. He's long dead. This is his son. Lupus Albus *Secundus*,
the White Wolf of Phrygia . . .
STRABO: OK, whoever he's the white wolf of, I'd like to ask him
to come down, so I can explain what I'm sure he will join me
in laughing at, as a regrettable but, *amusing*, error. You see:
we were engaged to perform tonight at the home of Marcus
Rufus Cronax, richest man in Rome.
TITUS: Yes, his house is across the street . . .
STRABO: As you so wisely note. And, in the rain, we, mistakenly,
found ourselves *here* . . .
TITUS: We were expecting another group, but they were delayed
by the rain.
STRABO: Delayed by the rain, were they.
TITUS: But they've arrived now . . .
STRABO: Another troupe of *actors*?
TITUS: No. Of priests.
STRABO: . . . Priests.
TITUS: . . . Who are now conducting the funeral service.

(Pause.)

STRABO: The funeral service.

TITUS: Yes. The most solemn last rites for lost Brothers in Arms of the Tenth African Legion.

(Pause.)

Which sacred rites you have profaned.

(Titus exits.)

STRABO: . . . *All* right . . . *Pelargon* . . .

PELARGON: Don't talk to me . . .

PHILIUS: Strabo: *are* we going to Sicily?

STRABO: *All right:* here's my plan. *Here* is my plan: We are, are we not? The valued, the beloved friends of who? Pelargon? Of who?

PHILIUS: Of who, Strabo . . . ?

STRABO: Of Marcus Rufus Cronax, richest man in Rome, who, at this very minute—

(Silence. At the entrance to the dungeon is Lupus Albus, the White Wolf of Phrygia, backed by Titus and two Centurions.)

Sir, sir? *We* are the beloved friends of your neighbor: Marcus Rufus Cronax. Richest—

LUPUS ALBUS: Centurion . . .

TITUS: Quiet before Lupus Albus.

(Titus exits. Pause.)

LUPUS ALBUS: Were you sent by Cronax? *Cronax* do you say?

STRABO: Yes, sir. Yes, sir. We are in the pay of Cronax.

LUPUS ALBUS: Sent by him?

STRABO: Yes!

LUPUS ALBUS: Cronax, our staunchest foe. In the Senate . . . ?

STRABO: He's in the "Senate," do you say?

LUPUS ALBUS: As all the world knows—

STRABO: All the world but us poor *actors*—ha ha ha, no—god forbid we get involved in politics . . .

LUPUS ALBUS: Indeed?

STRABO: Oh, please. We are as innocent of politics as the Babe Unborn.

LUPUS ALBUS: Then, you say, you do not know of our disgrace . . .

PHILIUS: I tried to tell you.

STRABO: Your disgrace? No. No. I know nothing but your interminable Career of Martial Glory! Oh, Mighty Scourge of . . .

PELARGON: Phrygia . . .

STRABO: Oh, mighty Scourge of Phrygia.

LUPUS ALBUS: And, you alone, in all Rome, are ignorant of our first defeat?

STRABO: "First *defeat*"? No.

PHILIUS: No, Strabo, you heard about that . . .

STRABO: The Tenth African Legion *fail*?

PHILIUS: Strabo, *you* know that . . .

STRABO: The young child is insane, and "we keep him *by* us, as a reminder of the fragility of all things."

LUPUS ALBUS: You did not know, we had been recalled to Rome to suffer disgrace and decimation before Caesar . . .

STRABO: May the gods decree otherwise . . . oh, sir . . .

LUPUS ALBUS: . . . which disgrace was ordained by that swine, *Cronax*? . . .

STRABO: . . . A curse upon his seed . . .

LUPUS ALBUS: . . . who stood in the Senate and demanded that decimation . . . to which we go at sunrise?

STRABO: May the sun, sir, which rises upon the disgrace of the Tenth African Legion live to rue the day.

(Pause.)

LUPUS ALBUS: Have you not uttered sufficient blasphemy.

STRABO: *"blasphemy"* . . .

LUPUS ALBUS: You have spewed your bawdy filth at the sacred observance of the Funeral Ode for Fallen Comrades.

STRABO: I plead to spend the remainder of my life in expiation.

(Titus enters. Men grumble offstage.)

TITUS: Sir, the men, in their rage, are clamoring for the actors' blood.

LUPUS ALBUS: Clamoring for blood are they? . . . Let's give them blood, then—to cleanse this vile blasphemy.

STRABO: Uh . . .

LUPUS ALBUS *(To Titus)*: Kill them all . . .

(Lupus Albus turns to go.)

STRABO: Wait, sir! Wait.

(Lupus Albus turns back.)

LUPUS ALBUS: My thoughts are elsewhere.

STRABO: Just the one moment, if I may.

(Pause.)

I am an *actor*, sir, whose life, at *best*, is a series of shams. We neither farm, nor hunt. We are debarred from bearing arms. By those who *toil* in the world we are despised. Except for that one moment, when we are permitted, on the stage, to make them laugh. Or cry. In sympathy. Not even with ourselves. Good, sir, but for that better being we impersonate. For we, ourselves, are nothing.

(Pause.)

And we have offended you: who bleed for the State. And should we, having wronged you, suffer at your hands: though, in our weakness, we may weep, in our deeper soul we know the punishment is just . . . Turn, turn, ye gods . . . your face now toward us—now away—howe'er your visage shines, your hand is on us all.

(Pause.)

LUPUS ALBUS: Your name, Actor.

STRABO: Sir, I am but Strabo.

LUPUS ALBUS: That speech . . .

STRABO: Sir . . .

LUPUS ALBUS: Is it not from *The Metathon* by *Plautus?*
STRABO: Your Honor's learning is outpaced only by his bravery.
LUPUS ALBUS: Yes. Thank you. How would you describe that speech?
STRABO: It is a humble plea for mercy.

(Pause.)

LUPUS ALBUS: You asked how you might make right your offense.
STRABO: Bid me, sir . . . and the tide shall obey the moon.
LUPUS ALBUS: My Tenth African Legion is to appear, tomorrow, before Caesar. In disgrace . . .
STRABO: May all the gods, in their combined omnipotence . . .
LUPUS ALBUS: . . . Indeed . . . Might you. On our *behalf* . . . *give* that speech. In our name. To Caesar? . . . *(Pause)* To plead for us.
STRABO: Give the speech . . . before Caesar? . . .
LUPUS ALBUS: *Yes.*
STRABO: *Plead* before *Caesar?*
LUPUS ALBUS: Yes.
STRABO: Sir, were I to live ten thousand lives, I could not wish, *in* them, for any greater honor . . .
TITUS: But, General.
LUPUS ALBUS: Yes, Titus.

(Titus takes Lupus Albus aside and whispers.)

(To Titus) What? *(Titus whispers some more. Pause)* Thank you.

(Lupus Albus, sadly, turns back to the troupe.)

I am reminded that under the rules of war, the audience with Caesar is closed.
STRABO: Closed. Oh no.
PELARGON: Closed, what does that mean? . . .
LUPUS ALBUS: Only the members of the summoned Legion may attend the Imperial Audience.
TITUS: General.

(Titus whispers to Lupus.)

STRABO: What is he saying . . .

LUPUS ALBUS *(To Titus):* . . . in what capacity?

(Titus whispers some more.)

(To Strabo) He has reminded me. Of the position of Auxiliary . . .

PELARGON: Auxiliary, what is that? . . .

LUPUS ALBUS *(To Titus):* But, that hasn't been employed in *years* . . . I doubt . . .

STRABO: We'll do it!

(Titus whispers to Lupus Albus.)

PELARGON: What is it?

LUPUS ALBUS: I am reminded that, as per our *charter*, should one, of his Own Free Will, pledge himself . . .

STRABO: We'll do it!

LUPUS ALBUS: . . . bare his breast, and pledge himself to the Tenth African Legion.

STRABO: We'll do it!

LUPUS ALBUS: He may be *inducted*, as Auxiliary Member.

STRABO: Count me in, count *us* in.

PELARGON: Don't do it.

STRABO: What do we have to do? . . .

PELARGON: Don't do it . . .

LUPUS ALBUS: Say the pledge, bare the breast, and suffer the Solemn Ceremonial Blow . . .

STRABO: . . . the Solemn Ceremonial Blow?

PELARGON: I told you.

STRABO: No, uh, Pelargon, explain to him why. *(To Lupus Albus)* "The Solemn Ceremonial Blow . . ." would not actually be the "thing," you know, and the kid's getting over a cold. So, to bare his breast . . .

LUPUS ALBUS: . . . which Blow may, by statute, "neither cause pain, nor draw blood."

STRABO: The Solemn Ceremonial Blow, as I was saying, is that blow I seek. Induct us then, O Fell Scourge of Phrygia, and let us plead your case before great Caesar!

LUPUS ALBUS *(Receiving the ceremonial sword)*: Kneel then and bare your breast.

PELARGON: I don't like it.

STRABO: It can't cause pain nor draw blood—you *sissy*.

(They kneel and bare their breasts.)

LUPUS ALBUS: "By the hilt of that sword which won Rome from the wilderness. The Legion forever." Say it.

ALL: "By the hilt of that sword which won Rome from the wilderness. The Legion forever."

(Lupus Albus touches the side of the sword to their chests lightly.)

LUPUS ALBUS: Arise, Auxiliary Members of the Tenth African Legion.

(They rise.)

STRABO: Oh, how the world shines new formed, to a member of this noble band . . .

LUPUS ALBUS: Enjoy your rest, my brothers. For tomorrow, you stand before Caesar. Unshackle them.

STRABO *(To Pelargon)*: Well, what did I tell you? You're always looking on the dark side . . . *(To Lupus Albus)* Oh, Great Praetor, Lupus Albus . . . White Wolf of Phrygia . . .

(He turns back to Pelargon, then to Lupus Albus again, but Lupus Albus and his men have gone.)

(To himself) Gaius Paulus, you're *better off* drowned, 'cause who's gonna be the favorite of Caesar? And the cork merchants in Sicily can hire Gaius Paulus, dead though he is which *may* improve his acting . . .

PELARGON: Don't defame the dead.

STRABO: Because tomorrow morning, *we*, Auxiliary Members of the Tenth African Legion . . .

(Titus enters with two other men in military attire.)

PELARGON: Who is this? . . .

TITUS: This here's the armorer . . .

(The Armorer's Assistant begins taking measurements. First Phili-us, then Pelargon, then Strabo.)

STRABO: Ah. Yes, my comrade, yes. The armorer, who, no doubt, has come to strike off our shackles.

TITUS: . . . who's come to measure you for your ceremonial attire . . .

PELARGON: Ceremonial attire?

STRABO: Our *armor*, Pelargon—*armor*—as befits Members of the Legion!

PHILIUS: . . . We get a suit of *armor*? . . .

ARMORER: Chest?

ARMORER'S ASSISTANT *(As he measures each of the men)*: Thirty-eight. Forty-one. Forty-six.

ARMORER: Waist?

ARMORER'S ASSISTANT *(Measuring)*: Twenty-nine. Thirty-eight. Forty-two.

ARMORER *(To Strabo)*: Watch that mead!!

STRABO *(Pats his belly)*: Well, you know . . .

PHILIUS: We get a suit of armor. Oh good!

TITUS *(To the Armorer)*: You forgot to do the neckpiece.

ARMORER *(Departing)*: They won't need the neckpiece.

TITUS: Oh, that's right.

PHILIUS: Why won't we need the neckpiece?

ARMORER *(Exiting)*: 'Cause if you're wearing the neckpiece, your head won't fit on the chopping block.

(The Armorers exit.)

STRABO: I think I'm missing something.

PELARGON: Why would they put our head on the chopping block?

TITUS: To chop off your head.

STRABO: Yes, thank you. Uh . . . *(To Titus)* Could you explain this to us?

TITUS: . . . *You* know.

PELARGON: Pretend we don't know, and tell us.

TITUS: Caesar . . . ?

PHILIUS: . . . Yes . . . ?

TITUS: . . . as you know, recalled the Tenth African Legion to *Rome* . . .

PHILIUS: . . . We know that.

TITUS: Because we suffered an inglorious defeat.

STRABO: Yes that's too bad.

TITUS: And in such cases . . .

PELARGON: . . . oh no.

TITUS: The offending Legion. Must choose amongst itself . . .

PHILIUS: Um-mmm . . .

PELARGON: Oh, no . . .

TITUS: . . . three members.

PHILIUS: Oh, that would be us!

TITUS: To be publicly beheaded.

(Pause. He exits.)

PHILIUS: But, if you chop off our heads, we'll *die* . . .

PELARGON: Will somebody shut that kid up.

Scene Three

Morning in the cell. The Herald passes outside the window.

HERALD:

>See how the headsman's scaffold on the grass
>Salutes the wakeful as night steals away
>Each knows though all forget that life must pass
>How fortunate the man who knows the day.

Bactrian Lynx Brand Opium. Lynx Brand Opium. Look for the shining eyes on every packet. Get high and stay high, with Bactrian Lynx Brand Opium. It'll get you through the *Rainy* seasons.

(Strabo pacing back and forth. The other two sitting in their cells. A rooster crows.)

STRABO *(To Pelargon)*: All right. Here's my plan: "Wake up, wake up, wake up. The kid has a tummyache." The guard: "Help help help, this lovely young lad is in agony . . ." So on . . . The guard comes in, we hit him on the head . . .

PELARGON: And then what?

STRABO: We dress up as the guard.

PELARGON: *We* dress up as the guard?

STRABO: Well, yes. *One* of us . . .

PELARGON: It's futile, Strabo. We're in a *dungeon.* Surrounded. By the best-armed, most ferocious, and angriest men in Rome. Who are they angry at? They're angry at *us.*

STRABO: Let's . . .

PELARGON: And, Strabo, I am angry at *you. I'm tired.* They're going to cut my head off in a half hour, and I don't feel well.

PHILIUS: I'm frightened, Strabo.

STRABO: Hush, my Secluded Vale of Acanthis. Would I let anything befall you?

PHILIUS: They're going to kill us, Strabo.

STRABO: Not while the Ichor of Imagination pulses through my veins.

PHILIUS: . . . And I wish I'd been better to you. What did you ask? I could have made you happy.

STRABO: Thank you.

PHILIUS: It's just that you're so *old.*

STRABO: Uh-huh.

PHILIUS: If you'd been *younger . . .*

STRABO: Hm.

PHILIUS: Or better looking . . .

STRABO: Yes . . . I've got to think . . .

(Titus enters.)

No, no, the hour is not yet at hand. *No* . . .

TITUS: Na, I've got some news. I've got some good news and some *bad* news.

PELARGON: . . . Tell us the news.

TITUS: Caesar has reconsidered. Your sentence has been *changed!*

STRABO: Our sentence has been changed. Oh, Zeus, oh, merciful Mars, God of War, who, in his wisdom . . . our sentence has been changed!

PELARGON: What's the *bad* news?

TITUS: That *is* the bad news.

PHILIUS: They were going to cut our heads off. What could be worse news than that?

TITUS: Caesar has decided you are not to have your heads cut off as that is too merciful a death.

PELARGON: What's he gonna do instead?

TITUS: You are to be castrated, and drawn and quartered.

(Pause.)

They hang you for about a half an hour, then, they cut you down, and cut out your entrails and put out your eyes, *then* . . .

STRABO: Yes, that's quite all right.

TITUS: No, then it gets interesting, they—

PELARGON *(Interrupting)*: Why did they change the sentence?

TITUS: *Caesar* . . .

STRABO: . . . Yes?

TITUS: Already incensed at the defeat of the Tenth African . . .

PELARGON: Yes, yes, we know that . . .

TITUS: Is further maddened by the loss, at sea, of the Troupe of Gaius Paulus. His favorite actors.

(Pause.)

STRABO: *Oh.*

PELARGON: What's the good news?

TITUS: The *good* news . . . *(Confidentially)* . . . is that I've *managed* . . . at some personal expense . . . *(Produces a goblet from under his cloak)* . . . to sneak you in *this* . . .

PELARGON: What is it?

PHILIUS: . . . It's a cup.

TITUS: It is a cup of wine. But, what is *in* the cup?

(Pause.)

PHILIUS: Wine.

TITUS: Yes, but what's in the wine?

STRABO: What's in the wine?

TITUS: Opium. There's enough opium in here to kill a horse. If *each* of you drinks just one *mouthful*, you'll be fine, when, when . . . *(Offers the cup to Strabo)*

PELARGON: I'd like my sip *now*, please.

STRABO: Wait, but, to quaff that cup would be tantamount to surrender . . .

TITUS: You bet.

STRABO: . . . Not while I have a plan.

PELARGON: I'd like my sip now, please.

STRABO: That's why, you see, *that's* why you never amounted to anything, Pelargon . . .

PHILIUS *(To Pelargon)*: You told me you never amounted to anything because Strabo held you back out of jealousy . . .

STRABO: Oh, how *cheap*, Pelargon. How tawdry. Who has shared good and bad with you for twenty years. *Now* it comes out. Now. Facing death. Yes, *take* your sip. *Quitter* . . . Yes. Face death as you faced life—*cravenly, abjectly*. Take your sip.

PELARGON: Thank you. I will! Gimme the cup.

(Ramus enters.)

RAMUS: By the gods.

STRABO: Yeah, by the gods. And what is the thought I will bear. To my death?

RAMUS: Good morning.

STRABO: Your ingratitude. No. I do not *need* the opium, to dull my senses. *You* have dulled my senses.

(Titus starts to exit.)

No, actually. I'll *take* the opium . . . thank you.

TITUS: Two sesterces . . .

STRABO: *What?*

TITUS: I can't give it to you for *nothing*. 'F I get caught, it's my *job* . . .

PHILIUS: Good morning, Ramus . . .

RAMUS: Good morning . . .

STRABO: I don't *have* two sesterces.

TITUS *(Takes back the cup)*: Sorry.

STRABO: Wait, wait, wait. Isn't there anything . . .

TITUS: Lend me the kid for one half hour.

STRABO: You want me to trade this child for the cup of opium?

TITUS: Yes . . .

PELARGON: *Done.* Philius . . . ?

TITUS: Thank you.

STRABO: No, wait . . .

PELARGON: Philius, this fellow wants to tell you some of his war stories . . .

STRABO: Yes, no, wait, that wouldn't be a good idea.

TITUS: Sounds like a good idea to me.

STRABO: Noo, you can't have the child.

TITUS: Why not?

STRABO: Uh . . . his virginity is pledged to the Goddess Demeter.

TITUS: His virginity is pledged to the Goddess Demeter . . . ?

STRABO: As I have said . . . but *this* man *(Referring to Pelargon)* skilled in the arts of love . . .

RAMUS: I can attest to that . . .

STRABO: . . . this man . . .

TITUS: Ramus . . . ?

RAMUS: Titus . . . ? You know when I got up this morning . . .

STRABO: Will you shut up. Why did they let you in? . . .

TITUS: Let him in? Do you know who this *is*?

PELARGON: No.

TITUS: This is Ramus, who fought with the Tenth African Legion in the snows.

PHILIUS: What were you doing in the snows?

TITUS: We were lost.

STRABO: You were in the Tenth African Legion . . . ?

TITUS: *In* the Legion? . . . He saved the life of Lupus Albus Primus, the *original* White Wolf of Sardinia, whose *son*, the White Wolf of Phrygia, is our general today.

STRABO: He saved the life of the general's father . . .

TITUS: Who, on his deathbed, yes, clasped to his bosom, his young son and said, "What e'er this soldier, Ramus, desires in life, my son, *grant* it to him."

STRABO: Hold on now, and slow it down, the White Wolf of Phrygia, is pledged to grant this old bum's wish? . . .

TITUS: . . . for anything under Heaven.

PELARGON: Do you think I could have that opium?

STRABO: BY ALL THE GODS AT ONCE—Good Ramus. Intercede for us, with Lupus Albus, that stern, though worthy, commander who holds our lives in his hand.

RAMUS: All right.

STRABO: Oh, thank you. Thank you.

RAMUS: But the one thing I came to tell you:

STRABO: *Yes?*

RAMUS: The coin you gave me . . .

STRABO: Yes?

RAMUS: . . . it's counterfeit.

STRABO: I'll make it right.

RAMUS: And I was concerned, that if you paid for a good luck charm with a bad *coin*, you might have Bad Luck.

STRABO: What truth there is in your words. *(To Titus)* Call your commander. To hear this good man's appeal. Oh, ye gods, who lovingly grant absolution to the deepest sinner. Thank you from one who has, yet again, unearned, received your grace.

RAMUS: I'll drink to that.

(Ramus grabs the goblet, drinks and falls down in a stupor. All stand around, looking at the fallen Ramus.)

PHILIUS: Oh, dear . . .

(Pause.)

TITUS: Did he drink it all?

PELARGON: Yes.

TITUS: There's enough opium in there to sedate a musk ox.

STRABO: A "musk ox," you say?

TITUS: As I have said.

STRABO: Could we get some more, please?

(Drumbeats.)

TITUS: Nope. We're out of time. There's the death drum.

(Drumbeats again.)

And so it's time for your execution. *(As he leaves the dungeon)* FALL BACK, AND CLEAR THE PATH OF THE CONDEMNED.

(The drumbeats continue.)

CAESAR, IN HIS MERCY, GRANTS THEM ONE LAST
MOMENT FOR REFLECTION.

PELARGON: . . . Well.

(Strabo comes downstage to orate.)

STRABO: "Yes, I have sinned. For I am mortal. And the gods know
that all mortals sin and so inform us, taxing the sinner with
that which he misnames Ill Fortune. But for its better name
is Justice. How find we ourselves upon this stranded shore?
The failure of a rope, whose loss split the sail? An inclement
conjunction of wind and the tide? A moment's folly inspiring
the youth to seek his fortune on the sea . . . Until co-merged
with that salt element, he knew himself unfitted for the regu-
larity of Earth. Which bore him. And, in a half a glass may
mourn him . . ."

(Pause.)

PELARGON *(Prompting)*: "See the Phoenicians' mass . . ."
STRABO: . . . Yes, yes, yes. "See the Phoenicians' mass upon the
mottled shore . . ."
OFFSTAGE VOICE OF A GUARD: Members of the Tenth Legion, pre-
pare to meet your doom!
PHILIUS: Strabo . . .
STRABO: Yes, good-bye, child.
PHILIUS: Good-bye.
STRABO: Perhaps we shall meet again. Beyond the river.
PHILIUS: I hope so, but . . .
STRABO: Yes. In that happy land . . .
PHILIUS: Yes, but . . .
STRABO: And look down to see the Critics writhe in Hell . . .
PHILIUS: Yes, there's just the one thing . . .
STRABO: What, child? Speak.
PHILIUS: You shouldn't have given the old man a fake coin.
TITUS *(Offstage)*: Helmets off, greet those who, for their com-
rades' sake, must suffer death!

PHILIUS: Because, if you'd given him a real coin, perhaps our luck would not have changed.

(Titus, the burly Guards and the Priest arrive, helmets off, and open the dungeon's gates.)

PRIEST: O Mighty Mars, prepare to receive unto your care, the mutilated bodies of these, your servants . . .

PHILIUS: Strabo . . .

GUARD: Are the condemned men prepared . . . ?

PHILIUS: Give him a coin, Strabo. Give the old man a coin.

STRABO: What?

PHILIUS: You cheated him of his coin for the good luck charm. Don't let that be on your soul, before . . . before . . .

(Philius weeps.)

STRABO: No, child, I would not die with that upon my soul. *(To Titus)* Give me a coin.

TITUS: Bind them, and hood them, and draw them forth.

STRABO: Give me a coin, for the love of God.

TITUS: Why should I give you a coin?

STRABO: Lend me a coin.

TITUS: You'll be dead in half an hour.

STRABO: Then you can take it *back* . . .

TITUS: No, that's good economics . . . *(Hands him a coin)* Just for the half hour, mind . . .

(Titus exits. Strabo hands the coin to Ramus.)

STRABO: Ramus, Ramus, wake up.

RAMUS: . . . what . . . ?

STRABO: Here's the coin I owe you.

(Pause.)

For the good luck charm? Ramus? For the *Good Luck* charm . . . ?

(Beat.)

RAMUS *(Waking)*: . . . the coin for the good luck charm.

(We hear a drum roll offstage.)

GUARD: It's time.

(The Guards begin to bind the three.)

PHILIUS: I'm sorry that I wouldn't go to bed with you, Strabo.
STRABO: That's all right.
PELARGON: I'm sorry that I *did* . . .
PHILIUS: And I regret I never knew the joy. Of acting with you. Onstage.
PELARGON: Imagine a toothache.
GUARD: Make way for the condemned!

(They engage in a group hug. The drum gives a final roll.)

STRABO *(To Philius)*: Good-bye, young lad, farewell, beauty.
PHILIUS: Good-bye, Strabo.
STRABO *(To Pelargon)*: Good-bye, old comrade.
PELARGON: I'm two years younger than you.
STRABO: But I've aged better.
PELARGON: Die with dignity.

(Pause.)

STRABO *(Sighs)*: Come, friends, let's show them how to make an exit . . .

(They start toward the door.)

TITUS *(Reentering)*: Great news, great news, great news! *(Beat)* The troupe of the actor Gaius Paulus, favorite of Caesar, believed lost at sea, has been found alive!
STRABO: The day lacked only *that* to be complete.
TITUS: In honor of which, Caesar has remitted punishment for all crimes. Up to, and including that, decreed for the Tenth Legion!!! *(Pause)* You are all free to go!!!

(Beat. Titus and the Guards exit the cell. Then the three actors start toward the door. Beat. Strabo turns back.)

STRABO *(To Pelargon, regarding Ramus)*: . . . Get the coin back.

Scene Four

Morning. The studio of Strabo. The Herald walks by outside the studio, in which we find Strabo and Philius.

HERALD:
> Oh Rome arise and welcome that new day
> The gods have decreed for our disport
> Work, frolic, suffer, sin and pray
> In the bright courtyard of the somber court
> Arise, ye nobles, citizens and slaves
> Some to dig gardens, others to dig graves,
> For whilst the sun . . .

STRABO *(Shouting out)*: Oh, not *today*, not *today*, *would* you please? Work is at hand, *love* is in the air, and nobody in a good mood ever listened to philosophy.

(A horn is heard, offstage.)

HERALD *(Going off)*:
> Hark to the Second Herald of the Morn
> The packet boat's departure horn

Make haste, make haste down to the quay
If you are bound for Sicelay . . .

STRABO: Oh, stuff a sock in it.

HERALD: Tunics and togas. Bernstein Brand Tunics and Togas. Made by philosophers: "They just wear on and on." Buy Bernstein Brand Tunics and Togas.

(The Herald moves off.)

STRABO *(To Philius)*: Continue.

PHILIUS *(Declaiming)*: ". . . What is more precious than wine, you ask? What is more precious than wine . . . ?"

(Pelargon enters with letters.)

PELARGON *(To Strabo)*: I've got the suitcases strapped up. *(Gesturing offstage)*

STRABO: One moment. *(To Philius)* Say it simply, like it's just *occurred* to you.

PHILIUS *(Nods)*: "What is more precious than wine . . . ? You *ask* me: I will tell you Cork."

STRABO: *Pause, pause,* Cork.

PHILIUS: I'm here to *learn.* You bid me, *whatever* you bid me, Strabo, *that* I shall do.

PELARGON: His father's late with the tuition.

STRABO: No matter. We'll be paid in *Sicily* . . . Keep it up, lad, keep it up.

PHILIUS: "What is more precious than wine? Mff mff. Cork . . . For without Cork, what *good* is wine? . . . Answer me that, good citizens of Sicily."

STRABO: That is it, my lad. *Look* them in the eye, and *make* them answer you that.

PHILIUS: God bless you, Strabo . . .

STRABO: And you, my little lamb.

PHILIUS: You are a wise mentor.

STRABO: Where, in this spotted life have I heard words as sweet? . . .

PHILIUS: I look forward to our time in Sicily.

STRABO: As do I, my amphora of honeyed mead.

PHILIUS: Will you teach me to swim?
STRABO: . . . You could call it that.

(There is a knock at the door.)

Ah—That would be the stevedores come for our baggage . . .
PHILIUS: I'll get it. "Haste then, young champion, to the Gate of
Acharnia, and report what messenger, and with what intent,
disturbs our disport . . ."

(Philius exits.)

STRABO *(To Pelargon)*: Well, he's willing, he's *young*, he's beautiful,
and perhaps he'll learn.
PELARGON: And perhaps the sun, in search of novelty, will rise in
the west.
STRABO: How ill your cynicism becomes you.
PELARGON: Really . . .
STRABO: I need a drink before the ship.

(They go off. Philius goes to the door.)

PHILIUS *(Opening the door)*: Welcome to the Studio of Strabo . . .
What errand brings you to our door? . . .
QUINTUS: I've come for the rent.
PHILIUS: Aha.

(Quintus enters with a letter, which he hands to Philius.)

QUINTUS: And the postman handed me this letter for your master.
PHILIUS: He and Pelargon have stepped out for a drink.
QUINTUS: How may they drink, being perpetually impoverished?
PHILIUS: They drink upon credit, sir. As we have been given an
engagement.
QUINTUS: An *engagement*?
PHILIUS: Sir, as I have said.
QUINTUS: Where?
PHILIUS: In a half hour we sail. To open the Sicilian Cork Festival.
QUINTUS: . . . You sail for Sicily . . .

PHILIUS: . . . That's where they're holding it.

(Ramus enters.)

RAMUS: By the gods . . .

QUINTUS *(To Philius)*: You're *leaving* . . . ?

RAMUS: Might anyone gain merit by giving an old soldier some wine . . .

(Strabo and Pelargon enter with a flagon.)

PELARGON: I'll share my wine with you, good soul. And then farewell.

RAMUS: Where are you off to?

STRABO: Sicily.

QUINTUS: You're going to Sicily?

STRABO: Fear not for your rent, O, font of avarice, it shall be *sent* to you . . . Yes, the Sicilians impressed by our status as Auxiliary Members of the Tenth African Legion have engaged us to open the Sicilian Cork Festival.

RAMUS: Everyone's going to Sicily . . .

(He drinks the wine.)

STRABO: What do you mean?

RAMUS: Down at the docks. The Troupe of Gaius Paulus. Has just been engaged. To open the Sicilian Cork Festival . . .

STRABO: What? . . .

PHILIUS *(Producing the letter)*: Oh, Strabo. The landlord brought you a letter.

PELARGON *(Takes the letter and reads)*: "Please accept our regrets. The untimely resurrection to life of the Troupe of Gaius Paulus has forced us to rescind your offer of employment. Thank you for your interest in our festival."

(Pause.)

STRABO: . . . They gave our spot to *Paulus* . . .

(Pause.)

QUINTUS: I . . .

STRABO: No, please. Please, *evict* us, Landlord. To die hungry in the streets cursed by the gods, whom, it seems, we have irremediably offended.

(Pause.)

QUINTUS: Then you won't be going to Sicily.

STRABO *(As to a child)*: It seems the Sicilians, mistaking Renown for Merit, have given our spot to Gaius Paulus . . .

PHILIUS: . . . That hack.

STRABO: Chide me, O Fortune. I remain your fool. Let years of effort in your service count for naught. Exalt mine enemies and grind, beneath your heel, your slave.

QUINTUS: I grieve to hear of your reversal.

STRABO: The loss is not mine alone, nay, but that of the denizens of Sicily, forever denied our performance.

PELARGON: The gods grant them forbearance.

STRABO: Had I but funds, O, ye Immortals. I would transport *my* troupe to Sicily, and challenge Paulus. By the gods, I would enter the pageant unpaid and unmask him before all the world, as a usurper.

QUINTUS: What a spectacle that would bid fair to be.

STRABO: As you so rightly note.

QUINTUS: Had you but funds.

STRABO: Had I but funds. But no. They praise the candle who need but ope' the shutters to behold the sun . . .

PHILIUS: Be strong, Strabo . . .

(Pause.)

QUINTUS: True worth is often overlooked.

STRABO: The wonder is it's ever remarked.

QUINTUS: Take the lad, for instance.

STRABO: . . . The lad . . .

QUINTUS: Yes. Might I talk with you a moment.

(Quintus draws Strabo outside for a moment, leaving Philius and Pelargon.)

PHILIUS: I would have liked to go to Sicily . . .

PELARGON: Yes.

PHILIUS: Strabo said he was going to teach me to swim.

PELARGON: No doubt.

PHILIUS: Pelargon, do you feel that I have talent?

PELARGON: Son, you have that which is far rarer than talent.

PHILIUS: What is that?

PELARGON: A cheerful outlook.

PHILIUS: Yes, but I'll have to go home now. And go into the myrrh business.

PELARGON: There'll always be a need for myrrh.

PHILIUS: Indeed. But now I'll never learn to act.

PELARGON: Son, it's a life of disappointment. Talent is overlooked, youth vanishes, and we mourn not only the caprices of fate, but our own willfully squandered opportunities. *(Pause)* But I've enjoyed our time together.

PHILIUS: Thank you, Pelargon.

(Strabo and Quintus reenter.)

STRABO: Recall the stevedores! Our bags to the boat. For we take ship for Sicily . . .

PHILIUS: For Sicily?

STRABO: The Troupe of Strabo is to perform at the Sicilian Cork Festival!

PELARGON: Where did the Troupe of Strabo get the money? . . .

PHILIUS: For Sicily? Oh, Strabo, hurrah! Hurrah!

PELARGON: Where did the Troupe of Strabo get the money? . . .

PHILIUS: Oh, Strabo, how I admire you!

STRABO: I hope, I sincerely hope, my acolyte, you, whose devotion has warmed, if not my nether parts, that higher portion of this earthly self.

PHILIUS: Your heart?

STRABO: Yes. You have warmed my heart, young Philius. And, lad, in Sicily . . .

PHILIUS: How did we get the fare for Sicily? . . .

STRABO: . . . The fare for Sicily . . .

PHILIUS: Yes.

STRABO *(Brings Quintus forward)*: *This* man, young Philius, this patron of the arts, has, in his unexampled generosity, funded our passage.

PELARGON: . . . Why?

STRABO: Nor is this all. He undertakes, young Philius, to continue your tutelage.

PHILIUS: My "tutelage"?

STRABO: Yes.

PHILIUS: . . . The landlord's coming with us to Sicily? . . .

STRABO: No, you're not going to Sicily. You're staying here.

PHILIUS: We're not going to Sicily?

STRABO: No, lad. Beautiful lad. I must go to Sicily, while you remain.

PHILIUS: Without *you*, Strabo . . . ?

STRABO *(Aside)*: Oh, break, my heart . . . *(To Philius)* Without me, yes, but *this* fine man . . . *(Referring to Quintus)* . . . is pledged to instruct you in the noblest of life's mysteries.

PHILIUS: The landlord's going to teach me to act?

STRABO: No, you're going into real estate.

RAMUS: In *this* market?

END OF PLAY

School

School was produced in September 2009 at Atlantic Theater Company (Neil Pepe, Artistic Director; Jeffory Lawson, Managing Director) in New York City. It was performed as a double bill with *Keep Your Pantheon*. It was directed by Neil Pepe. Set design was by Takeshi Kata, costume design was by Ilona Somogyi and lighting design was by Christopher Akerlind. The production stage manager was Gregory T. Livoti. The cast was as follows:

A	John Pankow
B	Rod McLachlan

Two people. An office.

A: The posters say: "I Will Protect My *Planet* . . ."
B: . . . Yes.
A: . . . "By Recycling Paper."

(Pause.)

B: Yes.
A: The hall is full of them.
B: Yes.
A: There are hundreds of them.
B: No, there are more than that.
A: How many more?
B: Each child did one. *(Pause)* That's why they're all different . . .
A: . . . They're all different.
B: . . . to express his or her . . .
A: "I Will Protect My Planet By Recycling Paper"?
B: Yes.

(Pause.)

A: Doesn't that use a lot of paper?

B: The posters are made on recycled paper.

A: The posters are made on recycled paper.

B: Yes. That was the students' idea.

A: *They* decided to use recycled paper.

B: For the *poster?*

A: Yes.

B: No. They *always* use recycled paper.

A: . . . *That's* the students' idea.

B: No. That's school policy.

A: Well, then, what was the students' idea?

B: The text.

(*Pause.*)

A: The *text:* "I Will Use Recycled Paper"?

B: Yes.

A: "I Will Save This Planet by Using Recycled Paper"?

B: Yes.

(*Pause.*)

Using it. Do you see?

A: No.

B: *Using* recycled paper. As, as, as . . .

A: . . . I . . .

B: . . . as an, not an "irony," but . . .

A: . . . All right . . .

B: As, they might say, as an *"in joke."*

A: . . . Yes . . .

B: About the project *itself.*

(*Pause.*)

As a self-referential comment.

(*Pause.*)

A: Why didn't they just save the paper?

B: There was no need to save the paper.

A: Why not?

B: Because it was recycled.

A: The "poster" paper was recycled.

B: Your *question* is: "Can it be recycled *again*?"

A: Yes. That's my question.

B: Of course.

A: "Of course it can."

B: Yes.

A: I . . . why "of course"?

B: It was recycled *before*.

A: But: I cannot conceive that it can be recycled *indefinitely*.

(Pause.)

Can it?

(Pause.)

Certainly, there must be some . . . "energy loss."

(Pause.)

Mustn't there?

B: Well, that's a question for the science teacher.

A: . . . Yes . . .

B: I would think, I would think *nothing* can be recycled *indefinitely* . . .

A: . . . No.

B: As there must be *some* "energy loss."

A: How *do* they recycle paper?

B: "How do they recycle paper," they . . .

A: They take it and "pulp" it, do they not?

B: They pulp it.

A: So *that*:

B: . . . They take it and pulp it.

A: So: even if they reused *all* of the old paper, there would . . .

B: They would have to use new "energy," yes. In the "pulping process."

A: . . . they would have to use new energy in the pulping process. *Such* energy having to have had to come from . . . from . . .

B: . . . Uh . . .

A: From "somewhere."

B: That's right.

A: For example, uh . . . "coal."

B: Yes.

A: Or, "water flowing over a *dam*."

B: Hydroelectric . . .

A: Yes. Or . . . yes, or burning trees *themselves*, which is to say, the burning of "wood." Or . . .

B: Or "oil."

A: Or "oil," certainly, but from some *nonrenewable resource*. To change the new thing. It is a principle of physics. That matter may not be created or destroyed.

B: Matter may not be destroyed?

A: No.

B: Why not?

(Pause.)

A: You're joking.

B: No.

A: It is not a *prohibition*. It is a *description*.

B: I don't understand.

A: I'm not suggesting "matter may not be destroyed" is a *prohibition*, such as, "This Washroom Is for Students Only." Or . . .

B: No, please, I understa . . .

A: Or, "No Smoking on School Property."

B: No, please, I understand you.

A: . . . But a "*description* of the physical world." A term I would define as "the way things are."

B: Matter may not be destroyed.

A: No.

B: Then where does it go?

(Pause.)

A: Where does it go "when"?

B: When we destroy it.

A: "When we destroy it."

B: Yes. As when we "burn" it. As when we burn paper. *You've* "burned paper."

A: It becomes ash.

B: But the *ash* . . .

A: Yes.

B: The *ash*. Must have less *volume*. Than the. The . . .

A: . . . the?

B: The *paper*.

(Pause.)

Mustn't it?

(Pause.)

A: What about the smoke?

B: The volume of the smoke and the ash equal the volume of the paper?

A: Matter may not be destroyed.

B: What about the firebombing of Dresden?

(Pause.)

Dresden was destroyed. Or if not, what happened to Dresden?

A: Dresden was destroyed.

B: Yes.

(Pause.)

And it wasn't even a strategic target.

A: Well. What difference if it was a strategic target or not. And, and . . .

B: I just . . .

A: AAAAND, *whether* or not it was a strategic target, would be a . . .

B: You're right.

A: . . . question.

B: You are correct.

A: For the history teacher.

(Pause.)

B: You're . . . WELL.

A: Yes.

B: But that just begs the question.

A: How so?

B: How so? *As*: the question is: what constitutes History?

A: *"History"* . . .

B: Yes.

A: As I understand it. Is, the Study of "What Happened."

(Pause.)

B: According to whom.

A: According to whom?

B: Yes.

(Pause.)

A: The Historians.

(Pause.)

B: And have they never made an error?

A: The Historians. Being *human*.

B: Yes. Of course.

A: Have "erred." The question is, *absent* Historians. How would we know what had occurred.

B: I . . .

A: Even *if* they were in error.

B: If they were *in error*, *then*.

A: . . . Yes . . .

B: AT A MINIMUM. We would be misinformed.

(Pause.)

A: That is correct.

B: With the attendant . . .

A: . . . Yes, but, BUT. BUT. How would we know that we are misinformed?

(Pause.)

Which is to say, in what "way" would it affect our lives?

B: We would be acting upon faulty information.

A: Yes, but we would not "know" it. As if. For example: a man. Is caught in an unhappy marriage. BUT IS UNAWARE OF IT.

B: If it were unhappy, how could he be unaware?

A: If, for example. If:

(Pause.)

B: If the sex were good.

A: Well, then, how could the marriage be unhappy.

B: IF, for example . . .

A: Yes . . .

B: The fellow.

(Pause.)

A: "If The Sex Were Good" would that not, not "indicate," but "establish" it was an unhappy marriage?

B: A "happy" marriage.

A: I beg your pardon. And, further, what "happens" to the paper. When it gets recycled?

B: They recycle it.

A: How?

(Pause.)

B: I don't know.

(Pause.)

That would be custodial services.

A: Are they the janitors?

B: Not anymore.

A: They *used* to be the janitors, yes?

B: That's right.

A: And *they* "recycle" the paper . . . ?

B: They take it to the recyclers.

A: They are "tasked" with taking it to the recyclers.

B: Yes.

A: And we don't "know" what the recyclers do.

B: No.

(Pause.)

A: Could we inquire?

B: Why?

A: So . . .

B: So we would "know" . . .

A: Yes.

B: Why would that be necessary?

A: Because. It *occurs* to me that, *perhaps*. A better *use* of the posters. Would be *to*: keep them. And, for example, "Cut them up into little cards," and use them for notepaper.

B: No, we . . .

A: For the secretaries.

B: No. We couldn't do that.

A: Why not?

B: You're kidding.

(Pause.)

A: No.

B: You're not kidding?

A: No. I'm serious.

(Pause.)

B: We . . .

A: "Cut up . . ."

B: Cut up. The work of *students*.

(Pause.)

We cut up the work of students.

A: Yes.

B: Based upon . . . ? Based upon what?

(Pause.)

Based upon what criteria?
A: That it was hanging on the wall.

(Pause.)

B: Because we'd have to . . . to destroy AND USE *ALL* of it.
A: For fear of . . .
B: That's right.
A: No. SO THAT. To *reuse* the, the . . .
B: "work"
A: could be said, not to be a sign of . . .
B: "disrespect . . ."
A: . . . of disrespect. But . . .
B: . . . Yes.

(Pause.)

A: "An endorsement"?
B: No.
A: No, it could hardly be "an endorsement" to cut the, the . . .
B: Students'.
A: To cut up the students' work. ON THE OTHER HAND.
B: This is why, *this* is why I . . .
A: No, you're right. We . . .
B: Leave it to the custodial staff.
A: Let *them* take it to the recyclers.
B: Yes.
A: That's something that we can be proud of.
B: To the extent they do.
A: Well, do they take it to the recyclers or not?
B: When they have the time.
A: What do they do when they don't have the time?
B: We do not inquire as to the *specific* uses of their time. As long as
the tasks are accomplished.
A: What if the tasks are not accomplished?

B: Well. The tasks will always be accomplished.

A: Be . . . ?

B: . . . because they set the tasks.

A: The janitors set the tasks?

B: Well. To whom would you give that responsibility?

A: They "set their own tasks."

B: Yes.

A: The "unions."

B: The "unions," who are made of *janitors*. Set the tasks for the janitors. Which is to say, for the custodians.

A: And what is the *difference*? Between a strategic, and a nonstrategic target?

(Pause.)

As we "won" the war.

B: Well, that's a narrow view.

A: A narrow view as its debatable if we won the war?

B: No, we "won" the war. Though, while not debatable, it is ironic. That the cars we drive. Are made by the nations we obliterated. That's ironic.

A: And I *wonder*. If child molesters. Should be forced to register.

B: How else would we know where they are?

A: Yes, but, dragging that chain. From one community, to the next. How could they restart their lives?

B: No one can restart his or her life.

A: Why not? Which, you will see, is a philosophical question.

B: Then let it be answered by philosophers.

A: They're using *paper*—to *discourage* waste. Eh? To *shame* those who *use* paper. And these "signs," for example: "This Washroom IS for the Students ONLY. No Adults Allowed."

B: Yes. That *itself* uses paper.

A: And doesn't that "sexualize" the young?"

(Pause.)

I wonder about that crossing guard.

B: Which one?

A: You know.

B: . . . Mmm.

(Pause.)

A: You see, this is the problem of *command.*
B: Mm.
A: To say *nothing.* Is to risk, um um . . .
B: Yes.
A: And become liable.
B: . . . Not if we didn't know.
A: Not if we didn't know, indeed.
B: As we *don't* know.
A: *While,* on the other hand, to "act" . . .
B: Is to risk injustice.
A: AND legal action by the union.
B: Not if it's true.
A: Well, curiously, *especially* if it's true.
B: How so?
A: As preliminary DENIABLE discussions have led to the deniable, suggesting that, were we to proceed, they might anonymously file charges against us for dereliction for not acting to remove an ongoing known menace.

(Pause.)

B: But how would they know that we knew?
A: We put up the sign.
B *(Sotto voce)*: But I thought they *allowed* the sign.
A: The janitors.
B: Yes.
A: They *suggested* the sign.

(Pause.)

I believed, at the time, it was a compromise. I see now it was a tactical ploy.
B: Those swine.

(Pause.)

A: Well. They're very political.

B: We could *bar* the crossing guard in question, from access to the campus.

A: The union won't allow it.

B: Why?

A: Unaccused, and unconvicted? It's a violation of his rights.

B: What about an "entrapment scheme"?

A: How would it work?

B: We take a *student* . . .

A: A "gay" student? . . .

B *(Sotto voce)*: . . . How do we know that they're "gay"?

A *(Sotto voce)*: Oh please . . .

B *(Sotto voce)*: Are we thinking about the same . . .

A: Well . . .

B: You know, I feel that many of these kids. Behave in a seductive and provocative way. Essentially, to torment the teachers.

A: . . . Um . . .

B: In effect, they're "cruising."

(Pause.)

Especially in the Lower School.

(A sighs.)

And, you turn around and "do" anything about it, and you spend the rest of your life in jail.

A: Not if it's not discovered.

B: Oh, it's all discovered. It all comes out. And, as I say, I wonder if that's not their *point*. The little *pigs*.

A: Well. I don't share your tastes, but I share your perception.

B: And I find their *dress* so provocative.

A: As who does not. *More* to the point: if we had a regulation, against making posters, we would save the paper, and the cost, both in material, and in worker hours. D'you think the teachers would allow it?

B: That's all they *do* is make posters. That's all they *do*. That's all they *do*. One month to the next. What else do they *do*? For the love of God? These budding *Einsteins*.

A: And bombing, I feel, based on no personal "knowledge," but "intuitively," must *usually* be a mistake.

B: How so?

A: As it must strengthen the resolve of the bombed.

B: Well. It might certainly *do* so.

A: Might? It certainly *must*. Imagine: crockery flying. The. The.

B: Accumulation.

A: The accumulation of *years*. Of bric-a-brac. Mementos.

B: Yes, that's certainly true.

A: *Plaques* that one accrues.

B: Mm-hmm.

A: For years of service.

B: . . . Yes.

A: One has to *dust* them. But one doesn't want some foreign *swine*. Raining down ordnance upon one's *treasures*.

(Pause.)

And what about the *ink*?

B: The ink?

A: The *poster* ink. The *ink* came from somewhere. There was a cost for the *ink*. In energy. And resources.

B: But: If we did not expend resources . . .

A: Mmm . . .

B: *In* the poster. *In* the paper. *In* the ink . . .

A: Mmm-hmm . . .

B: And even on the *sign* . . .

A: . . . All right.

B: . . . How would we transmit *information*?

END OF PLAY

David Mamet is the author of many plays, including *Glengarry Glen Ross* (Pulitzer Prize, 1984), *American Buffalo, The Cryptogram, A Life in the Theatre, November, Boston Marriage, Speed-the-Plow, Oleanna, Race, The Anarchist* and *The Woods*.